It's all about …

POLAR
PLUNGE

KINGFISHER
NEW YORK

KINGFISHER
LONDON & NEW YORK

Copyright © Macmillan Publishers International Ltd 2016
Published in the United States by Kingfisher,
175 Fifth Ave., New York, NY 10010
Kingfisher is an imprint of Macmillan Children's Books, London
All rights reserved.

Distributed in the U.S. and Canada by Macmillan,
175 Fifth Ave., New York, NY 10010

Library of Congress Cataloging-in-Publication data
has been applied for.

Series editor: Sarah Snashall
Series design: Little Red Ant
Adapted from an original text by Philip Steele

ISBN 978-0-7534-7262-0

Kingfisher books are available for special promotions
and premiums. For details contact: Special Markets
Department, Macmillan, 175 Fifth Ave.,
New York, NY 10010.

For more information, please visit
www.kingfisherbooks.com

Printed in China

9 8 7 6 5 4 3 2 1

1TR/1115/WKT/UG/128MA

Picture credits
The Publisher would like to thank the following for permission to reproduce their material.
Top = t; Bottom = b; Center = c; Left = l; Right = r
Cover Shutterstock/AndreAnita; Back cover Shutterstock/Sofia Santos; Pages 2–3,
30–31 Shutterstock/Volodymyr Goinyk ; 4–5 Kingfisher Artbank; 5b Shutterstock/Polina
Melnyk; 6, 6c Shutterstock/Tyler Olsen; 7 Shutterstock/outdoorsman; 8 Corbis/Yi Lu;
8b Shutterstock/Photick; 9, 9t Shutterstock/Natalia Davidovich; 10 Shutterstock/
idreamphoto; 10b Shutterstock/Vlada Z; 11 Shutterstock/FloridaStock; 12 Shutterstock/
Delmas Lehman; 12b Shutterstock/Paul Reeves Photography; 13, 32 Shutterstock/
outdoorsman; 13b Shutterstock/Nadezhda Bolotina; 14 FLPA/PhotoResearchers;
15t Arcticphoto/B&C Alexander; 15b Shutterstock/3355m; 16 Getty/Imagno; 17 Getty/Sue
Flood; 17b Corbis/Bettman; 18 Shutterstock/Volodymyr Goinyk; 19t Shutterstock/Denis
Burdin; 19b Corbis/George Steinmetz; 20 FLPA/Minden Pictures/Flip Nicklin;
20b Shutterstock/Dmytro Pylypenko; 21 Shutterstock/bikriderlondon; 21t, 31 Shutterstock/
nice_pictures; 22 Alamy/Photos 12; 23 Flickr/Recuerdos de Pandora; 23b Corbis/Reuters;
24 Corbis/Galen Rowell; 24b Flickr/Daniel Leussler; 25 Shutterstock/MarcAndreLeTourneux;
26 Corbis/George Steinmetz; 27 Corbis/Denis Sinyakov; 28–29 Arcticphoto/B&C Alexander.
Cards: Front tl FLPA/Minden Pictures/Flip Nicklin; tr Shutterstock/FloridaStock;
bl Shutterstock/Josef Pittner; br Shutterstock/Tsepova Ekaterina; Back tl Flickr/Christopher
Michel; tr, bl Shutterstock/Dmytro Pylypenko; br FLPA/Minden Pictures/Flip Nicklin.

Front cover: A polar bear walks on top of the Arctic ice.

CONTENTS

For your free audio download go to
www.panmacmillan.com/audio/
PolarPlunge **or** goo.gl/rHlGMJ
Happy listening!

The ends of the Earth

If you travel very far north or very far south, you will reach the wild, beautiful lands of ice and snow. These are the polar regions.

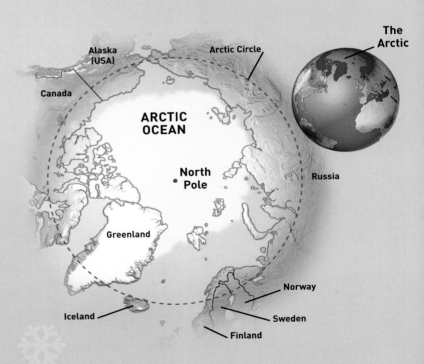

Alaska (USA)

Arctic Circle

Canada

ARCTIC OCEAN

North Pole

Greenland

Russia

The Arctic

Norway

Iceland

Sweden

Finland

The North Pole is the most northerly place on Earth. The area around the North Pole is called the Arctic Circle.

The South Pole is the most southerly place on Earth. The area around the South Pole is called the Antarctic Circle.

FACT ...

The word "Arctic" comes from the Greek word, *arktikos*, which means "near the bear."

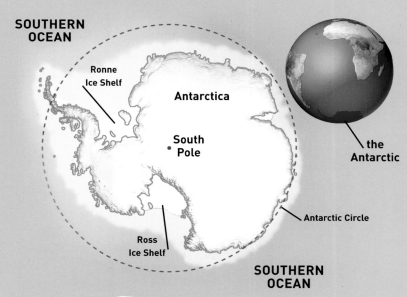

SOUTHERN OCEAN

Ronne Ice Shelf

Antarctica

South Pole

the Antarctic

Antarctic Circle

Ross Ice Shelf

SOUTHERN OCEAN

Penguins live on the ice and rocks of Antarctica.

The big freeze

The Poles are covered with ice all year long. During winter, slabs of floating sea ice form and icebergs break off from glaciers.

It is difficult to see anything in an Antarctic blizzard.

People on a polar expedition during a snowstorm.

In the middle of the polar summer, it stays light even at night. In the middle of the polar winter, it stays dark all day long.

FACT ...

The world's lowest known temperature of minus 138.5 degrees Fahrenheit (–94.7 degrees Celsius) was recorded in Antarctica in 2010.

A group of walruses rest on an Arctic ice floe.

The frozen North

There is no land underneath the North Pole—it is an area of frozen ocean and moving ice. Farther south, the ice melts each summer and freezes again each winter. The Arctic Ocean is surrounded by land covered in plains—called tundra—and mountains.

The ice near the North Pole never melts.

Icy mountains covered by snow drifts lie on the coast of Greenland.

Grasses, mosses, and wildflowers grow on the tundra in summer.

No trees can grow here because deep down the soil remains frozen all year long.

tundra mushrooms, plants, and moss

FACT ...

The most northern patch of land on Earth is an island called Kaffeklubben in Greenland.

Home of the polar bear

Many animals live in the bitter cold of
the Arctic: plankton, fish, birds, whales,
and the mighty polar bear—the top
hunter of the Arctic.

A humpback whale
leaps out of the water.

Arctic cod have chemicals
in their bodies that prevent
them from freezing.

Record breaker:	largest land-based carnivore
Length:	up to 10 ft. (3m)
In danger from:	melting ice cap
Eats:	seals

A polar bear and her cub roam the ice hunting for seals.

FACT ...

Polar bears have an amazing sense of smell and can locate a seal from more than a mile (1.5km) away!

Back to life

When summer arrives and the snow melts, the Arctic tundra comes alive with flowers, insects, and animals that arrive for the summer.

Snow geese spend their summers feeding on grasses on the tundra.

Whimbrels migrate to the tundra to breed in summer.

Many animals leave the tundra at the start of winter, but some remain. The Arctic fox stays. Its fur is brown in summer and white in winter for camouflage.

The Arctic fox only gets cold when the temperature is less than −94 °F (−70 °C.)

Thousands of caribou travel up to 3000 miles (about 5000 kilometers) to spend the summer on the Arctic tundra.

Peoples of the Arctic

People settled on the land around the Arctic Ocean thousands of years ago.

They learned the skills needed to survive in the harsh climate. They wore skins and furs to stay warm and were expert at fishing and hunting seals.

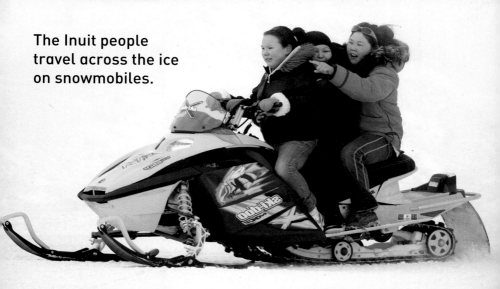

The Inuit people travel across the ice on snowmobiles.

FACT ...

Reindeer herders hold spring festivals where there is reindeer racing, reindeer lassoing competitions, and snowmobile races.

Arctic explorers

In 1893, Fridtjof Nansen let his ship, the *Fram*, drift into the pack ice. After drifting for 18 months he tried to reach the North Pole on skis, but the journey was impossible.

Fridtjof Nansen's team

SPOTLIGHT: Fridtjof Nansen

Lived:	October 10, 1861 to May 13, 1930
Record breaker 1:	went "farthest north"
Record breaker 2:	first crossing of Greenland
Award winner:	won the Nobel Peace Prize

Explorers have reached the North Pole using snowmobiles, dog sleds, skis, and even parachutes.

Tourists from all around the world at the North Pole.

In 1909, Robert Peary claimed to have reached the North Pole, but not everyone believes he made it there.

South to Antarctica

Antarctica is a huge continent. It is made up of a solid mass of land and a number of islands. Most of Antarctica is buried under an enormous sheet of ice that is almost one and a half miles (two kilometers) thick.

Antarctica is a polar desert crossed by a jagged range of mountains.

There is very little tundra in Antarctica. Other than mosses and lichens, not many plants can survive here.

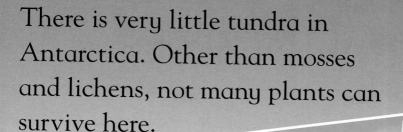

Glaciers extend out into the ocean forming ice shelves along the coast.

FACT ...

Mount Erebus is an active volcano in Antarctica. It creates smoking towers in the ice.

Land of the penguin

Life is only possible in the Antarctic around the coasts where the oceans are a rich source of food.

In the ocean there are plankton, krill, fish, leopard seals, Weddell seals, killer whales, blue whales, and colossal squid.

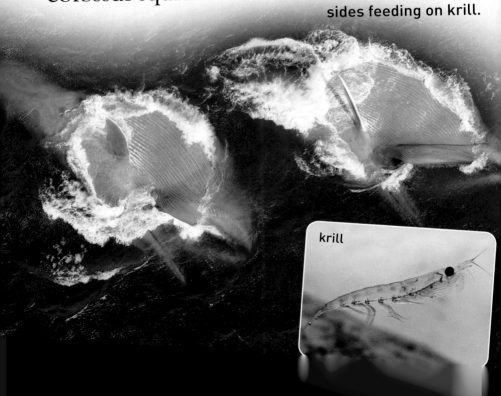

Two blue whales on their sides feeding on krill.

krill

FACT ...

The Arctic tern travels about 43,000 miles (70,000 kilometers) as it migrates between the Antarctic and the Arctic each year.

Five species of penguin live in Antarctica. These birds cannot fly but they are speedy swimmers.

SPOTLIGHT: Emperor penguin

Record breaker:	lives in harshest climate
Length:	3.8 ft. (1.15m)
In danger from:	global warming
Eats:	krill, fish, squid

Race for the Pole

In 1910, Norwegian explorer Roald Amundsen sailed to Antarctica. He used dog sleds and skis to travel over the snow and ice.

Amundsen and his team reached the South Pole on December 14, 1911.

SPOTLIGHT: Roald Amundsen

Lived:	July 16, 1872 – unknown
Record breaker 1:	crossed Northwest Passage
Record breaker 2:	first to reach the South Pole
Record breaker 3:	reached North Pole by airship

A British expedition led by Captain Robert Scott arrived at the South Pole just a few weeks after the Norwegians in January 1912. On the return journey the British team died in an awful blizzard.

Scott's expedition team

Scott's expedition hut, with much of its contents still intact, in the Antarctic.

Ice stations

No one has ever made a permanent home in Antarctica because of the harsh conditions. Scientists stay at research stations that can survive winds of 190 mph (300km/h).

Amundsen-Scott
South Pole Station

The Antarctic mainland does not belong to any one nation and there are strict limits on who can visit.

Scientists in Antarctica measure the ice. They study the rocks, the plants, the coastal animals, the weather, and the thickness of the ice.

Each year, a limited number of tourists are allowed to visit the Antarctic.

Warming up

Scientists studying ice and weather in the polar regions warn us that the ice sheets are becoming thinner and the sea ice is melting.

The ice is melting because of global warming. A big melt could cause low-lying islands and coasts all around the world to be flooded.

Dirty gases from factories and power stations in the Arctic contribute to global warming.

FACT ...

If scientists drill out ice from the ice sheet, they can find out what the climate has been like over the past 500,000 years!

The future

Polar bears, walruses, and penguins will all struggle to survive if the ice keeps melting.

If the sea ice disappears, more and more ships will be able to pass through the Arctic Ocean. Mining and oil companies want to move into new areas of the Arctic to extract valuable minerals and oil.

The Inuit way of life
depends on the survival
of Arctic wildlife.

FACT ...

In 2010 there was so little sea ice in the Arctic
that two boats managed to sail around the edges
of the Arctic Ocean for the first time in history.

GLOSSARY

blizzard Strong wind that carries snow.

camouflage Patterns or colorings that make an animal blend in with its surroundings.

climate The typical weather conditions in an area.

continent One of the world's seven largest masses of land.

glacier A deep, frozen river that moves very slowly.

global warming The heating-up of the layers of air around Earth.

ice floe A sheet of ice floating in an ocean or river.

iceberg A large block of ice that has broken off from a glacier or ice shelf.

Inuit The local people who live in or near the Arctic regions of the world.

migrate To travel long distances in search

of places to breed or feed.

North Pole The most northerly point on the planet.

pack ice Large pieces of ice that float in the ocean.

plankton Tiny plants and animals that float in the ocean.

polluted Poisoned or made dirty with waste.

snowmobile A motor vehicle used to cross ice or snow.

South Pole The most southerly point on the planet.

species A group of animals or plants that can breed together.

tundra An open region of the Arctic or Antarctic with very few trees. Tundra is frozen in winter, but the surface soil melts in summer.

INDEX